EXPLORING THE CANADIAN ARCTIC

Plants and Animals of the North

by Heather Kissock

and Leia Tait

Weigl

Published by Weigl Educational Publishers Limited
6325 10 Street SE
Calgary, Alberta
T2H 2Z9

www.weigl.com
Copyright ©2010 WEIGL EDUCATIONAL PUBLISHERS LIMITED

Library and Archives Canada Cataloguing in Publication

Plants and animals of the north.

(Exploring the Canadian Arctic)
Includes index.
ISBN 978-1-55388-960-1 (bound).--ISBN 978-1-55388-964-9 (pbk.)

1. Plants--Canada, Northern--Juvenile literature.
2. Animals--Canada, Northern--Juvenile literature.
I. Series: Exploring the Canadian Arctic (Calgary, Alta.)

QH106.2.A7P53 2009   j578.09719   C2009-903467-0

Printed in the United States of America
1 2 3 4 5 6 7 8 9 0 13 12 11 10 09

Project Coordinator: Heather Kissock
Design: Terry Paulhus

All of the Internet URLs given in the book were valid at the time of publication. However, due to the dynamic nature of the Internet,
some addresses may have changed, or sites may have ceased to exist since publication. While the author and publisher regret any
inconvenience this may cause readers, no responsibility for any such changes can be accepted by either the author or the publisher.

Every reasonable effort has been made to trace ownership and to obtain permission to reprint copyright material. The publishers
would be pleased to have any errors or omissions brought to their attention so that they may be corrected in subsequent printings.

Weigl acknowledges Getty Images as its primary image supplier for this title.
Gerry Mussgnug: page 7 bottom.

We gratefully acknowledge the financial support of the Government of Canada through the Book Publishing Industry Development
Program (BPIDP) for our publishing activities.

Contents

Beyond 60 Degrees

The Canadian North is a vast area that covers more than 40 percent of the country's total land. Nunavut, the Northwest Territories, Yukon, and the northern tip of Quebec make up this northern area.

Any land in Canada above 60 degrees latitude is considered the North. This imaginary line became the border of the northern region when Saskatchewan and Alberta were declared provinces in 1905.

Canada's North is made up of three main biomes. These are the Arctic tundra, the boreal forest, and **polar** seas. The region has flat lands, mountains, hills, and valleys, along with several major seas off its coasts. These are Baffin Bay, Davis Strait, the Arctic Ocean, Hudson Bay, and the Beaufort Sea. Since it is a polar region, the North has a dry, cold climate. Winter can last up to 10 months, with severely cold temperatures.

Even though this cold, dry environment would seem to hinder growth, the North is actually rich in life. Unique plants are found there, including some that do not grow any other place on Earth. Many animals find essential food and shelter in the region's varied **habitat**, and its microscopic ocean life has a major impact on the global environment. The North is truly a unique living world.

■ The ringed seal is one of the many animals that live in the cold Arctic environment.

Natural History of the North

Millions of years ago, Earth's ocean floor lifted and folded upon itself, forming the rocky islands of the polar seas. Over time, sea levels rose and fell. Waters repeatedly flooded and drained what is now northern Canada, building up layers of sandstone.

During the last **Ice Age**, about 17,000 years ago, massive sheets of ice flattened the land. These sheets, called glaciers, covered almost all of what is now Canada. They slid over the land on a thin layer of melted water, breaking down mountains, carving valleys, and scraping away rocks, trees, and soils.

Arctic wetlands are found mainly in the southern part of the region. They consist of bogs, fens, swamps, marshes, and shallow open water.

About 10,000 years ago, the Ice Age ended. Glaciers shrunk until only the places nearest the North Pole remained covered in ice. Even with the glaciers gone, however, ground in many parts of the North stayed permanently frozen. **Lichens** were the only life that could grow there. As the lichens took hold, died, and slowly decayed, their remains turned into soil. Eventually, flowering plants began to grow in the soil, and treeless tundra spread across the frozen earth. Lichen-eating animals, such as caribou and hares, moved north. Wolves and other predators followed, and the tundra **ecosystem** developed.

South of the tundra, water left behind by the melting glaciers created many wetlands. Mosses grew, and insects bred. In the drier places between wetlands, seeds carried by wind and birds took root. The region's first trees grew up in clumps across what is now Yukon, the southern Northwest Territories, and parts of Nunavut. Soon, these thickets became forests of spruce, pine, fir, and tamarack trees. Forest and wetland animals, such as moose, bears, and birds, moved in.

BERINGIA

During the last Ice Age, so much water was frozen in massive glaciers that sea levels dropped by as many as 150 metres. Land that was once covered by seawater became exposed. In the North, a land bridge appeared in what is now the Bering Strait. The bridge connected parts of present-day Russia, Alaska, and Yukon. Scientists call this ancient land Beringia.

Beringia had a very dry climate. Glaciers never formed there, even during the Ice Age. Instead, hardy grasses, herbs, and other meadow-like plants thrived. When the Ice Age ended, many of these plants continued to grow in Yukon. As the tundra and boreal forest developed, new plants grew alongside these Ice-Age survivors. As a result, Yukon has many unique plants. More than 30 species grow only in Yukon and parts of Alaska. These include Yukon Draba, Scotter's Draba, Ogilvie Spring Beauty, and Maclean's Goldenweed. Most of these species grow in northern Yukon, but scientists recently began finding new species in the southern parts of the territory, too.

Northern Biomes

The boreal forest, Arctic tundra, and polar seas shape life in the Canadian North. Plants and animals vary depending on which zone they inhabit. Their needs, abilities, appearance, and life cycles change with the landforms and climate of each zone. To understand these differences, it is important to see where these zones are located and how they relate to each other.

ARCTIC OCEAN
The Arctic Ocean is the smallest ocean in the world. It surrounds the North Pole and many islands in the Canadian North. More than 60 percent of the ocean is covered with ice all year long.

TREE LINE
The tree line marks the northern limit of the boreal forest and the beginning of the Arctic tundra. Trees do not grow north of the tree line. The tree line is not straight, since trees grow at different latitudes, depending on changes in climate.

BOREAL FOREST
The boreal forest covers 2.5 million square kilometres of Canada. It stretches more than 5,000 kilometres from Yukon to Newfoundland and extends 1,000 kilometres south from the tree line. In the North, the boreal forest covers most of Yukon and southern parts of Nunavut and the Northwest Territories.

LEGEND
- Arctic Tundra
- Boreal Forest
- Tree Line

Arctic Ocean

Beaufort Sea

U.S.A.

YUKON

NORTHWEST TERRITORIES

BRITISH COLUMBIA

ALBERTA

SASKA

U.S.A.

GREENLAND

Baffin Bay

Davis Strait

NUNAVUT

Hudson Bay

MANITOBA

WAN

ONTARIO

QUEBEC

Life in the Boreal Forest

In the boreal forest of the North, thick belts of evergreen trees rise above soft carpets of moss and lichen. These treed areas are linked by numerous muskegs, cold grassy bogs that produce **peat**. Winters are long and cold, with little snow. Summers are short and cool, with plenty of rain. These conditions give rise to the unique plant life that defines the region.

Early Explorers

Many early travellers in the Canadian North were unprepared for the long, harsh winters. When their food supplies ran out, some turned to eating lichens, which they nicknamed "*tripe de Roche*", or "rock tripe."

June 9, 1884
"Had nothing but tripe de Roche, tea, and sealskin gloves for dinner. Without fresh bait we can do little in shrimping, and so live on lichens and moss alone."

June 10, 1884
"The stewed tripe de Roche today was delicious, having boiled it for the first time. It leaves a sweetish taste in the mouth."

– A. W. Greely,
Cape Sabine, Ellesmere Island, 1886

The boreal forest of Canada's North is made up mainly of conifers, such as spruce, pine, balsam fir, and tamarack trees. The most northern point of the boreal forest reaches the Mackenzie River Delta in the Northwest Territories. There, the trees are smaller and grow farther apart than in the southern parts of the region.

In places that are thick with conifer trees, moss completely covers the ground. Sphagnum is the most common species. In bogs and muskegs, each layer of sphagnum grows over the next, and the dead layers never fully decay. This half-rotted material is the main ingredient in peat.

Throughout the boreal forest, tree trunks and open sections of ground are covered with lichens. Lichens are the main food eaten by caribou and other animals that winter in the boreal forest.

Many mammal species are found in the North's boreal forest. Moose thrive in the cool climate and live in the forest year round. They are often found near muskegs and fresh waters, where they swim and graze. Barren-ground caribou migrate to the forest in winter to feed on the plentiful lichens. Both moose and caribou are hunted by black bears, wolverines, and grey wolves. Other predators, such as lynx, hunt smaller species of animals, including beavers, muskrats, hares, and red squirrels.

Throughout the year, birds come and go in the North's boreal forest. Some stay year-round, while others migrate to the area in the summer to mate. In the North, it is common to see cranes, geese, ducks, loons, and gulls on the water. Many birds of prey, such as hawks, owls, eagles, and Peregrine falcons, can be found hunting small mammals.

Birds are able to survive by feeding on smaller animals that also reside in the area. These include several varieties of fish, such as lake trout, pike, whitefish, and salmon, that live in the lakes, rivers, and streams scattered through the forest. Frogs and toads also provide birds, and other animals, with a food source. Some birds even feed on the insects, including mosquitoes and black flies, that gather around the area's muskegs and wetlands.

■ The moose is the largest member of the deer family. It is an herbivore, which means it eats only plants.

■ Lynx are nocturnal animals. This means they are active mainly at night.

CONIFER TREE FEATURES

Most conifer trees share the same basic features. They grow between 18 and 25 metres tall, and their trunks are very straight. The shortest branches are at the very top of the trunk, forming a point. Moving down the trunk, each layer of branches is a bit longer than the last, creating a cone shape. The branches themselves are covered in narrow, green needles, while the lower section of the trunk is bare.

Tundra Plants and Animals

With its lack of trees, the Arctic tundra is sometimes called a polar desert. However, it is home to more than 2,000 species of land plants. These plants have adapted to life in the cold, dry climate of the North. Most grow in clusters close to the ground to avoid the wind. Many are covered with fuzz to help them keep warm.

Each July, the tundra is hidden under a thick carpet of wildflowers, such as the mountain avens. As an adaptation to the harsh Arctic climate, the mountain avens has light-coloured petals that reflect heat to the dark centre of the flower, where growth occurs. The mountain avens moves its flower to track the Sun across the sky. This allows it to absorb as much sunlight as possible and keep warm.

Shrubs, such as the Arctic willow and mountain cranberry, have adapted to life in the North. The small Arctic willow lays flat against the ground, absorbing heat from the dark soil. Mountain cranberry has thick leaves that allow it to store water without losing moisture through its leathery skin.

■ The mountain avens is a member of the rose family of flowers. It was named the territorial flower of the Northwest Territories in 1957.

Like Arctic plants, animals that live on the tundra have adapted to the cold climate. Many Arctic mammals grow very large, which helps them stay warm. They often have thick, dense fur that insulates them from the cold. As food can be scarce on the tundra, many Arctic animals have adapted to eat whatever they can find. This means they eat a wider variety of foods than their relatives in warmer climates. Despite these challenges, there are many animals that live on the Arctic tundra, especially during the summer.

By facing outwards, the huddled muskoxen are ready to charge at their predators if necessary.

Barren-ground caribou range across the mainland. Caribou have thick fur coats to keep them warm. They survive by eating lichens, moss, and other plants found in the area.

Caribou share the land with the muskoxen. These shaggy animals have thick hair that hangs to the ground. Underneath the hair is a fleecy undercoat that keeps them warm. Muskoxen huddle together to keep warm and to protect themselves from predators, such as the Arctic wolf.

Very few birds spend the winter on the tundra. However, some, such as snowy owls and ptarmigans, live in the region year round. Both birds are able to keep warm due to their thick feather coverage. Unlike most birds, snowy owls and ptarmigans are completely covered by feathers, even on their beaks and feet.

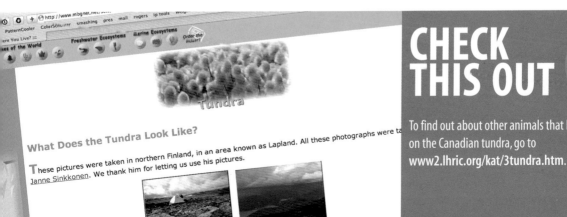

What Does the Tundra Look Like?

These pictures were taken in northern Finland, in an area known as Lapland. All these photographs were ta[...] Janne Sinkkonen. We thank him for letting us use his pictures.

CHECK THIS OUT

To find out about other animals that live on the Canadian tundra, go to www2.lhric.org/kat/3tundra.htm.

Life in the Arctic Seas

Seas in temperate climates are usually teeming with different types of **algae**. The polar seas, however, are covered in ice for most of the year. This surface ice prevents **photosynthesis**, which is necessary for algae to grow. Still, some algae have adapted to these harsh conditions.

The majority of the algae in the Arctic Ocean and surrounding waters are diatoms. These are single-celled algae that live in Arctic sea ice. They collect in tiny spaces between ice crystals and in salty water inside the ice. Diatoms live off the Sun's energy. This means that, in winter, there is barely enough light for them to survive. During spring and summer, they grow rapidly along the side and bottom of sea ice chunks, and in open water. They are important food for **zooplankton**, worms, fish, birds, and seals.

■ Polar bears are solitary animals, except when mating or raising cubs.

While large colonies of algae in the Arctic seas are very limited, the waters are home to some of the most unique animals in the world.

The polar bear is one of the Arctic's top predators. It is the largest land carnivore on Earth. Though the polar bear lives on land, it is known as the "bear of the sea." It can swim very well, dive as deep as 3 metres underwater, and stay submerged for up to two minutes. Polar bears are sometimes seen on the tundra, but they prefer to spend their lives roaming the Arctic ice and swimming in the cold ocean. With their thick blubber to keep them warm, they are uniquely built to survive the frigid waters of the Arctic Ocean.

Ian Stirling

Ian Stirling, one of the world's leading experts on polar bears, is a senior research scientist with the Canadian Wildlife Service and a professor of zoology at the University of Alberta. He has written a number of books and research articles on polar bears.

"No one just walks past a polar bear, even if he or she has seen hundreds before; every single bear is special and worthy of special appreciation."

The ringed seal is the polar bear's main prey. The smallest of all seals, it tends to avoid predators by living mainly in the water and on sea ice. It rarely ventures onto land. Females even give birth to their pups on the ice. They build a snow cave to hide from their predators while raising their young.

The narwhal is a small whale that lives in the Arctic's rivers and coastal waters. The males have a long, protruding tooth that looks like a horn growing from their head. For this reason, they are sometimes called the "unicorn of the sea." Like the polar bear, this unique animal has a thick layer of blubber that provides insulation from the cold.

A narwhal's tooth can be up to 2.7 metres long.

DIATOMS AND CLIMATE CHANGE

Diatoms are found in waters all around the world. All diatoms are highly sensitive to climate change. If the water temperature changes by even a few degrees, the type, size, and number of diatoms found in the water can change dramatically. For this reason, scientists interested in climate change often study diatoms. Recently, scientists studied the remains of diatoms at the bottom of many Arctic lakes. They found that the diatoms in these lakes had changed a great deal over the last 150 years. The types of diatoms that once lived there are now gone and have been replaced by new species. This indicates that lakes across the Arctic are warming. Scientists believe this is the result of pollution in the atmosphere.

Web of Life

All of the plants and animals in a biome depend on one another for survival. Everything contributes something to its environment and takes something to survive. Each animal gives and takes in just the right amounts so that the biome stays in balance.

Each living thing belongs to a food chain. Food chains form when an animal eats a plant or another animal. Energy moves from the **organism** that is eaten to the organism that eats it. A food chain diagram shows the direction that energy, in the form of food, is passed from one living thing to another. The arrows show the direction in which the energy moves.

Each of the biomes in Canada's North has distinct food chains. These chains are unique to the different animals and plants that live in each biome. However, animals and plants may belong to more than one food chain, depending on what they eat and what eats them.

OCEAN FOOD CHAIN

Polar Bear

Cod

Seal

Plankton

Algae

U.S.A

YUKON

NORTHWEST TERRITORIES

BRITISH COLUMBIA

ALBERTA

SA

U.S.A

LEGEND
- Arctic Tundra
- Boreal Forest
- Tree Line

cean

GREENLAND

Baffin Bay

Davis Strait

NUNAVUT

TUNDRA FOOD CHAIN

Arctic Fox

Lemming

Grasses and Lichens

Hudson Bay

BOREAL FOREST FOOD CHAIN

Lynx

Weasel

Squirrel

Nuts, berries

MANITOBA

'AN

ONTARIO

QUEBEC

Habitat Loss

Though most of the Arctic is untouched by humans, it still faces many concerns from human activity. Global warming, pollution, and land development projects pose a threat to the plants and animals living north of 60.

Climate change poses a severe threat to the survival of life forms in the Arctic. Scientists estimate that Arctic sea ice may disappear within the next 70 years. In the past 20 years, Arctic ice has retreated about five percent, posing a huge threat to polar bears in particular. These massive marine mammals walk along the ice to hunt seals that live there. Without the ice, the bears cannot reach their prey, and the seals have no place to live. As well, walruses require thick sea ice to rest on while they feed. Arctic sea ice has lost 30 percent of its thickness in recent years, making it more challenging for walruses to find ice that will support their weight.

■ Oil production in the Arctic is contributing to the pollution in the area. Besides the toxins being put in the air, there is also the risk of oil spills. These can contaminate both water and land.

Though very little pollution is created by the people living in the Arctic, the region is at threat of pollutants from other parts of the world. For example, air and ocean travel creates pollutants. As well, chemicals travel to the area via river currents. Animals that drink from these waters or eat plants that have been nourished by them can become ill. In fact, pesticides and other **toxins** have been detected in the body tissue of some Arctic animal species, such as seals. In nature, the Sun's rays help break down pollutants. Since Arctic areas receive less sunlight, pollutants take longer to break down.

■ Walrus live and raise their young on the sea ice. As the ice melts in the south, adults are moving farther north, leaving their young behind to fend for themselves.

Land development is greatly affecting the habitat of northern plants and animals. Mining operations, road construction, testing areas for bombs, and housing projects are just some of the ways Arctic lands are now being used. This is of special concern in coastal areas where many animals breed. Caribou migrate to coastal regions to give birth and to live in the summer months. There is limited land remaining for these activities, and this is having a negative impact on the caribou population.

■ Mining operations disrupt plant growth and take habitat away from animals.

The Changing Face of the Arctic

Millions of years ago, the Arctic looked very different than it does today. Fossil discoveries show that flying lemurs and other tropical animals roamed the land. The area was also lush with tropical vegetation. However, threats, such as climate change and hunting, caused most of these plants and animals to become extinct. Today's Arctic species began to populate the area following the last Ice Age. Many are similar to plants and animals found in more southern locations. They have, however, had to adapt to the much colder climate.

THEN	NOW
SUMMER	
Animals lived in constant daylight for part of the year. During this time, a hippo-like animal called Coryphodon ate flowering plants, **deciduous** leaves, and water-based plants.	Arctic summer is short with nearly constant sunlight. The growing season is short, and plants reach only about ankle high. Animals must use this brief season to breed and forage enough food to survive the long winter.
WINTER	
Animals lived in constant darkness for the remainder of the year. During this period, Coryphodon ate twigs, fungi, leaf litter, and coniferous needles since plants likely went into hibernation to survive the cold.	Since water is frozen in winter, many fish-eating animals migrate to warmer areas in search of food. Those that remain in the tundra eat snow in place of water.
MAMMALS	
Tapirs, flying lemurs, and a rhino-like animal known as brontothere roamed the Arctic and may have originated in the region.	Warm-weather mammals have been replaced by polar bears, killer whales, and Peary caribou that have thick layers of blubber or dense fur to keep them warm.
REPTILES AND AMPHIBIANS	
Alligators and turtles frequented Arctic waters.	Reptiles can no longer survive the frigid temperatures. However, some amphibians, such as frogs and toads, have adapted to the region.
CLIMATIC CHANGES	
Tree stumps the size of washing machines have been found, indicating the land consisted of swampy forests. Studying these finds has shown scientists that the area likely had warm, humid summers and mild winters that rarely dipped below freezing.	Arctic land is permanently frozen, and temperatures remain below freezing for most of the year. Above the treeline, there are no trees and few plant species.

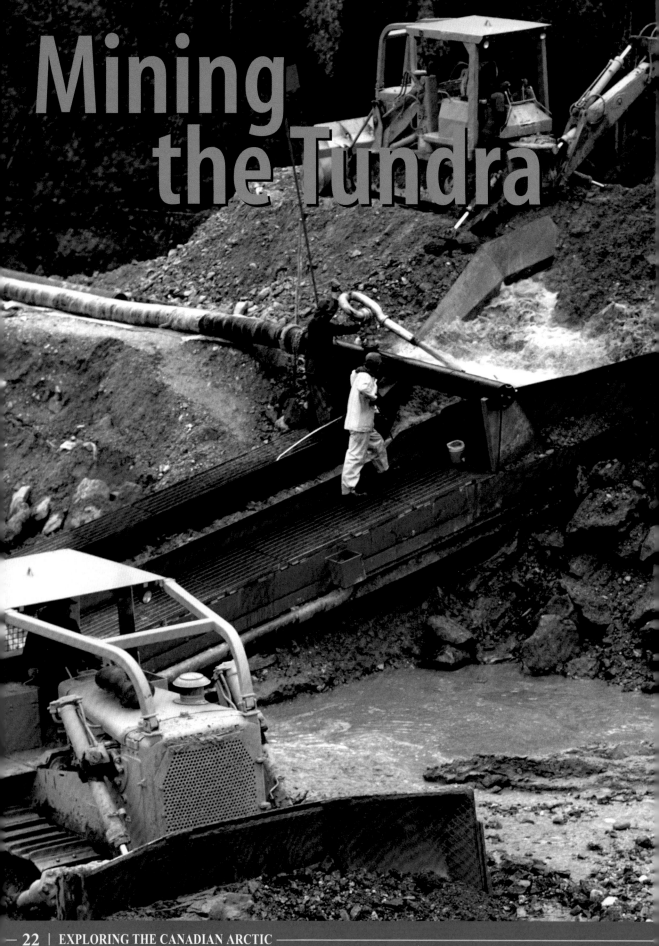

Mining the Tundra

AT ISSUE

Under its layers of snow and **permafrost**, the Arctic tundra is rich in natural resources, including gold, silver, lead, zinc, diamonds, oil, and natural gas. Gold and diamond mining are already important industries in the North, and many people want to build more mines. Others are very interested in drilling for oil and natural gas below the tundra and the ocean floor. These activities could earn a great deal of money for the North and for Canada.

Scientists are concerned about the impact these activities will have on the environment. The tundra is very fragile. Even the smallest event can have a major impact. For example, a single tire track can destroy a cluster of plants that have been growing for hundreds of years. Using heavy equipment to construct mines, roads, and buildings could severely harm the permafrost.

Any change to the permafrost could have a drastic effect on the tundra's ecosystem. Plant and animal life is so closely connected that a small change in either could easily upset the food chain. Damage to a patch of grass could harm the insects, small mammals, and birds that eat it, as well as the larger predators that rely on those animals for food.

Should mining be allowed in Canada's North?

A debate occurs when people research opposing viewpoints on an issue and argue them following a special format and rules. Debating is a useful skill that helps people express their opinions on specific subjects.

1. Decide how you feel about the issue described.

2. Ask a friend to argue the opposing viewpoint.

3. Use the information in this book and other sources to prepare a two-minute statement about your viewpoint.

4. Present your argument, and listen while your friend gives his or her argument. Make notes, and prepare a response.

5. Present your rebuttal and a final statement. Let your friend do the same. Did your friend's arguments change how you feel about this issue?

Animals in Peril

A s humans begin leaving their mark on the North, the way of life for the plants and animals that live there is being jeopardized. The Committee on the Status of Endangered Wildlife in Canada (COSEWIC) reviews the condition of all plant and animal species in Canada. Its scientists determine if a species is endangered.

BELUGA WHALE

The beluga is a small, white whale with a rounded head. It resides mainly in the eastern part of Hudson Bay. However, over the past 20 years, its population has decreased by about 50 percent. Scientists predict the beluga may be extinct in 10 to 15 years. Its decline is due to overhunting and habitat destruction.

WHOOPING CRANE

The whooping crane is named for its loud call, which can be heard from several kilometres away. Habitat destruction caused the near extinction of these birds. In 1941, there were only about 20 whooping cranes in the world. Today, due to conservation efforts, the birds number at almost 500.

IVORY GULL

The ivory gull is recognized for its pure white plumage. It has a stocky body similar to a pigeon, but is quite agile in the air. The ivory gull is found in the far reaches of the North. Over the past 20 years, its population has decreased by about 80 percent. This has been caused mainly by pollutants in its food chain.

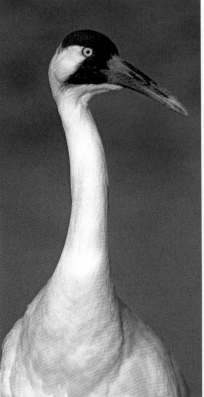

COSEWIC currently lists several species in the North as endangered. Many more are threatened, or at risk of becoming endangered.

RED KNOT

This shorebird migrates to Canada's North every year to breed. Over the past 15 years, its population has declined by 70 percent. Some of this decline is due to the overfishing of its main food source, the horseshoe crab. Other causes for its decline include global warming and pollution.

ESKIMO CURLEW

Scientists are unsure if this bird still exists in the North. The last confirmed Eskimo curlew nest was found more than 100 years ago. In the 1800s, this brown shorebird's population was estimated to be in the millions. However, due to overhunting, its numbers seriously declined. Still, sightings of the bird have been made in recent years.

PEARY CARIBOU

The Peary caribou is a forager, meaning that it grazes on plants for food. Due to climate change, the population has experienced an 84 percent decline over the last 40 years. The increasing warmth of the North melts the snow, which then refreezes into ice and covers the plants the caribou rely on for food.

Finding Sanctuary

3
Mountain Goat

Global warming and industrial development are bringing great change to Canada's northern environment. This is having a direct impact on the plants and animals found there. Populations are dwindling, and many species are struggling to survive. In order to save species from extinction, the federal and territorial governments have set aside land to act as wildlife preserves and sanctuaries. These areas are meant to protect animals and their habitats so that they can exist for future generations. Following are just some of the North's protected areas.

1 BYLOT ISLAND BIRD SANCTUARY
Area: 11,067 square kilometres
Special features:
- entire island was declared a sanctuary in 1965
- nesting area for the world's largest colony of snow geese
- became part of Sirmilik National Park in 1999

2 KENDALL ISLAND BIRD SANCTUARY
Area: 623 square kilometres
Special features:
- established in 1961
- only preserve located on Mackenzie Delta, one of the world's most significant bird breeding areas
- home to more than 90 bird species, including snow geese, and several mammal species

3 KLUANE WILDLIFE SANCTUARY
Area: 4,000 square kilometres
Special features:
- established in 1942
- was 26,000 square kilometres until 1972, when 22,000 square kilometres became Kluane National Park instead
- home to more than half the Yukon's mountain goat population

4 POLAR BEAR PASS NATIONAL WILDLIFE AREA
Area: 4,345 square kilometres
Special features:
- designated a national wildlife area in 1986
- supports more than 30 species of birds
- named for the polar bears that pass through the area every spring and summer

5 QUEEN MAUD GULF BIRD SANCTUARY
Area: 61,765 square kilometres
Special features:
- established in 1961 as a migratory bird sanctuary
- contains the largest variety of geese in any nesting area in North America
- nesting area for almost all of the world's Ross goose population

6 THELON GAME SANCTUARY
Area: 52,000 square kilometres
Special features:
- established in 1927 to preserve muskoxen populations
- most remote wildlife refuge in North America
- accessible only by canoe

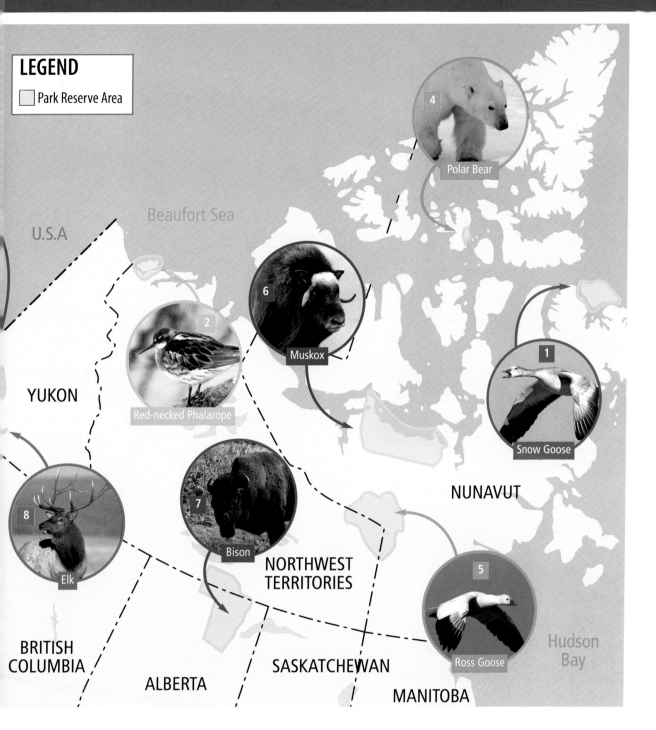

LEGEND

☐ Park Reserve Area

U.S.A

Beaufort Sea

YUKON

NORTHWEST
TERRITORIES

NUNAVUT

BRITISH
COLUMBIA

ALBERTA

SASKATCHEWAN

MANITOBA

Hudson
Bay

Polar Bear

Muskox

Red-necked Phalarope

Snow Goose

Elk

Bison

Ross Goose

7 WOOD BUFFALO NATIONAL PARK
Area: 44,807 square kilometres
Special features:
- Canada's largest national park
- created in 1922 to protect free-roaming bison
- became a **World Heritage Site** in 1983

8 YUKON WILDLIFE PRESERVE
Area: 3.4 square kilometres
Special features:
- first established in the 1960s by private individuals
- purchased by the Yukon Territorial Government in 2003
- home to 10 species of northern mammals, including muskoxen and Rocky Mountain elk

Quiz

What have you learned about plants and animals in the North? Take this quiz to find out.

1 When did the last ice age end?

2 What is the northern limit of the boreal forest called?

3 Cold, grassy bogs that produce peat are called what?

4 How many species of land plants are found on the Arctic tundra?

5 Why are many tundra plants covered in tiny hairs, or fuzz?

6 How have snowy owls adapted to their northern climate?

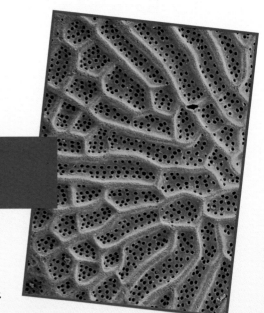

7 What ice algae are important indicators of climate change?

8 Which Arctic animal is the largest land carnivore in the world?

9 What are three threats to animal and plant habitats in Canada's North?

10 Identify three endangered animals in Canada's North.

curlew, Peary caribou
10. Whooping crane, beluga whale, ivory gull, red knot, Eskimo
9. Global warming, pollution, and land development
8. The polar bear
7. Diatoms
and feet
6. By growing feathers all over their body, including their beak

warm
5. To keep warm
4. More than 2,000
3. Muskegs
2. The tree line
ago
1. About 10,000 years ago
Answers:

Blubber Bags

Blubber helps keep marine mammals warm in cool water. The following activity shows how blubber keeps animals warm.

What you will need
- ice
- cold water
- bucket
- gloves made from a variety of materials, such as rubber, cotton, wool, or neoprene
- stopwatch
- thermometer
- lard or shortening
- sandwich bags
- tablespoon
- paper towel
- packing tape

1. Scoop a large amount of lard or shortening into a sandwich bag.

2. Turn another sandwich bag inside out. Place this bag inside the bag that is filled with the lard or shortening. Make sure the tops of both bags line up.

3. Use a paper towel to wipe the tops of the bags clean. Then, tape the bags together. Leave a small opening for your hand.

4. Fill the bucket with water. Use the thermometer to measure the water temperature. Add ice until the temperature is between 9 and 18 degrees Celsius.

5. Place your bare hand in the ice water. How long can you keep your hand in the water? Repeat the experiment wearing different gloves. Finally, place your hand inside the blubber bag. How long can you keep your hand in the water? Which bag keeps your hand the warmest? Why?

Further Research

Many books and websites provide information on the North. To learn more about plants and animals in the North, borrow books from the library, or surf the Internet. Most libraries have computers that connect to a database for searching for information. If you input a key word, you will be provided with a list of books in the library that contain information on that topic. Nonfiction books are arranged numerically, using their call number. Fiction books are organized alphabetically by the author's last name.

Books

Banting, Erinn. *Tundras*. New York, NY: Weigl Publishers Inc., 2006.

De Medeiros, Michael. *The North*. Calgary, AB: Weigl Educational Publishers Limited, 2006.

Miller-Schroeder, Patricia. *Boreal Forests*. New York, NY: Weigl Publishers Inc., 2006.

Websites

Learn everything you need to know about hundreds of Arctic species at **www.arctic.uoguelph.ca/cpl**.

Research plant life, animals, and ecosystems of the North at Hinterland Who's Who at **www.hww.ca**.

Take an Arctic eco-quiz at **www.ecokids.ca/pub/eco_info/topics/climate/adaptation_quiz**.

Watch animal videos, download images, and listen to the sounds of the boreal forest at **www.borealkids.org**.

Glossary

algae: plantlike organisms that do not have stems, roots, and leaves

deciduous: trees that lose their leaves at the end of the growing season

ecosystem: a community of living things sharing an environment

habitat: the environment in which a plant or animal lives and grows

Ice Age: a period in which a large part of Earth was covered in ice

lichens: plant-like organisms formed by algae that live inside fungus

organism: anything that is alive, such as a plant, animal, or fungus

peat: dark brown or blackish soil made from partly decayed plants and water; when dried, it is sometimes used as fuel or fertilizer

permafrost: part of the ground that is frozen year round

photosynthesis: the process green plants use to change water and carbon dioxide into food for themselves

polar: at, near, or relating to either of Earth's poles

toxins: poisonous substances

World Heritage Site: a place designated by the United Nations to have cultural signficance on a global level

zooplankton: tiny animal life that floats in water

Index